POEMS
1968–1970

ROBERT GRAVES
POEMS 1968-1970

CASSELL · LONDON

CASSELL & COMPANY LTD
35 Red Lion Square, London, WC1
Melbourne, Sydney, Toronto
Johannesburg, Auckland

First published 1970

I.S.B.N. 0 304 93634 0

Printed by The Camelot Press Limited,
London and Southampton
F. 670

FOREWORD

Collected Poems 1965, in sections numbered from I to
XVIII, had superseded five similar collections since
1926, each in turn rejecting a large number of pre-
vious choices in favour of new ones. This was followed
by *Poems* 1965–1968 in sections numbered from XIX
to XXII, and here is *Poems* 1968–1970, the sections
continuing to XXV. There is a further section of
occasional verse. Having more to say, no continued
need to earn my living by writing historical novels,
and fewer children around my knees, has for some
years now swelled the yearly number of poems I
write, though each must still go through a long series
of drafts before being either suppressed or accepted on
probation. In one's seventy-fifth year it is easy to
plagiarize oneself, but I have done my best to weed
such plagiarisms out; no legitimate pack of cards
should contain more than one Jack of Diamonds or
Ace of Hearts.

Poets have for centuries used the childbirth meta-
phor of a poem's appearance after difficult labour.
Yet, just as in true childbearing the mother has
admitted alien genes to her blood-stream, a tolerance
markedly affecting her thoughts, desires and be-
haviour throughout gestation, so also in the poet's
birth-metaphor. The poem of which he is brought to
bed must have alien genes: borrowed, at the best, from
the woman with whom he is in love, and at the worst
from the whore of contemporary fashion.

Deyá 1970   R.G.

CONTENTS

XXIII

XXIV

XXV

OCCASIONALIA

XXIII

SONG: DREAM WARNING

A lion in the path, a lion;
A jewelled serpent by the sun
Hatched in a desert silence
And stumbled on by chance;
A peacock crested with green fire,
His legs befouled in mire;
Not less, an enlacement of seven dreams
On a rainbow scale returning
To the drum that throbs against their melodies
Its dark insistent warning.

SONG: BEYOND GIVING

There is a giving beyond giving:
  Yours to me
Who awoke last night, hours before the dawn,
  Set free
By one intolerable lightning stroke
  That ripped the sky
To understand what love withholds in love,
  And why.

SONG: THE SIGIL

Stumbling up an unfamiliar stairway
   Between my past and future
And overtaken by the shadowy mind
   Of a girl dancing for love,
    I glanced over my shoulder.

She had read my secret name, that was no doubt,
   For which how could I blame her?
Her future paired so gently with my own,
   Her past so innocently,
    It flung me in a fever.

Thereupon, as on every strange occasion,
   The past relived its future
With what outdid all hopes and fantasies—
   How could I not concede
    My sigil in its favour?

SONG: BASKET OF BLOSSOM

Jewels here lie heaped for you
Under jasmine, under lilac—
Leave them undisclosed awhile;
If the blossoms be short-lasting
Smile, but with your secret smile.

I have always from the first
Made my vow in honour's name
Only thus to fetch you jewels,
Never vaunting of the same.

SONG: YESTERDAY ONLY

Not today, not tomorrow,
Yesterday only:
A long-lasting yesterday
Devised by us to swallow
Today with tomorrow.

When was your poem hidden
Underneath my pillow,
When was your rose-bush planted
Underneath my window—
Yesterday only?

Green leaves, red roses,
Blazoned upon snow,
A long-lasting yesterday,
Today with tomorrow,
Always and only.

SONG: TWINNED HEART

Challenged once more to reunite,
    Perfect in every limb
But screened against the intrusive light
    By ghosts and cherubim,

I call your beauty to my bed,
    My pride you call to yours
Though clouds run maniac overhead
    And cruel rain down pours,

With both of us prepared to wake
    Each in a bed apart,
True to a spell no power can break:
    The beat of a twinned heart.

SONG: OLIVE TREE

Call down a blessing
On that green sapling,
A sudden blessing
For true love's sake
On that green sapling
Framed by our window
With her leaves twinkling
As we lie awake.
Two birds flew from her
In the eye of morning
Their folded feathers
In the sun to shake.

Augury recorded,
Vision rewarded
With an arrow flying
With a sudden sting,
With a sure blessing,
With a double dart,
With a starry ring,
With music from the mountains
In the air, in the heart
This bright May morning
Re-echoing.

SONG: ONCE MORE

These quiet months of watching for
An endless moment of once more
May not be shortened,

But while we share them at a distance,
In irreproachable persistence,
Are strangely brightened.

And these long hours of perfect sleep
When company in love we keep,
By time unstraitened,

Yield us a third of the whole year
In which to embrace each other here,
Sleeping together, watching for
An endless moment of once more
By dreams enlightened.

SONG: THE PROMISE

While you were promised to me
But still were not yet given,
There was this to be said:
Though wishes might be wishes,
A promise was a promise—
Like the shadow of a cedar,
Or the moon overhead,
Or the firmness of your fingers,
Or the print of your kisses,
Or your lightness of tread,
With not a doubt between us
Once bats began their circling
Among the palms and cedars
And it was time for bed.

SONG: VICTIMS OF CALUMNY

Equally innocent,
Confused by evil,
Pondering the event,
Aloof and penitent,
With hearts left sore
By a cruel calumny,
With eyes half-open now
To its warped history,
But undeceivably
Both in love once more.

SONG: TO A ROSE

Queen of Sharon in the valley,
Clasp my head your breasts between:
Darkly blind me to your beauty—
Rose renowned for blood-red berries
Ages earlier than for fragrant
Blossom and sweet hidden honey,
Save by studious bees.

SONG: THE CLOCKS OF TIME

The clocks of time divide us:
You sleep while I wake—
No need to think it monstrous
Though I remain uneasy,
Watchful, albeit drowsy,
Communing over wastes of sea
With you, my other me.

Too strict a concentration,
Each on an absent self,
Distracts our prosecution
Of what this love implies:
Genius, with its complexities
Of working backwards from the answer
To bring a problem near.

But when your image shortens
(My eyes thrown out of focus)
And fades in the far distance—
Your features indistinguishable,
Your gait and form unstable—
Time's heart revives our closeness
Hand in hand, lip to lip.

SONG: WHEREVER WE MAY BE

Wherever we may be
There is mindlessness and mind,
There is lovelessness and love,
There is self, there is unself,
Within and without;
There is plus, there is minus;
There is empty, there is full;
There is God, the busy question
In denial of doubt.

There is mindlessness and mind,
There is deathlessness and death,
There is waking, there is sleeping,
There is false, there is true,
There is going, there is coming,
But upon the stroke of midnight
Wherever we may be,
There am I, there are you.

XXIV

GOLD CLOUD

Your gold cloud, towering far above me,
Through which I climb from darkness into sleep
Has the warmth of sun, rain's morning freshness
And a scent either of wood-smoke or of jasmine;
Nor is the ascent steep.

Our creature, Time, bends readily as willow:
We plan our own births, that at least we know,
Whether in the lovely moment of death
Or when we first meet, here in Paradise,
As now, so years ago.

COMPACT

My love for you, though true, wears the
    extravagance of centuries;
Your love for me is fragrant, simple and millennial.
Smiling without a word, you watch my extravagances
    pass;
To check them would be presumptuous and
    unmaidenly—
As it were using me like an ill-bred schoolboy.

Dear Live-apart, when I sit confused by the active
    spites
Tormenting me with too close sympathy for fools,
Too dark a rage against hidden plotters of evil,
Too sour a mind, or soused with sodden wool-bales—
I turn my eyes to the light smoke drifting from
    your fire.

Our settled plan has been: never to make plans—
The future, present and past being already settled
Beyond review or interpretative conjecture
By the first decision of truth that we clasped hands
    upon:
To conserve a purity of soul each for the other.

TRIAL OF INNOCENCE

Urged by your needs and my desire,
I first made you a woman; nor was either
Troubled by fear of hidden evil
Or of temporal circumstance;
For circumstances never alter cases
When lovers, hand in hand, face trial
Pleading uncircumstantial innocence.

LOVE GIFTS

Though love be gained only by truth in love
Never by gifts, yet there are gifts of love
That match or enhance beauty, that indeed
Fetch beauty with them. Always the man gives,
Never the woman—unless flowers or berries
Or pebbles from the shore.
                                    She welcomes jewels
To ponder and pore over tremblingly
By candlelight. 'Why does he love me so,
Divining my concealed necessities?'
And afterwards (there is no afterwards
In perfect love, nor further call for gifts)
Writes: 'How you spoil me!', meaning: 'You are
   mine',
But sends him cornflowers, pinks and columbine.

MANKIND AND OCEAN

You celebrate with kisses the good fortune
Of a new and cloudless moon
(Also the tide's good fortune),
Content with July fancies
To brown your naked bodies
On the slopes of a sea-dune.

Mankind and Ocean, Ocean and mankind:
Those fatal tricks of temper,
Those crooked acts of murder
Provoked by the wind—
I am no Ocean lover,
Nor can I love mankind.

To love the Ocean is to taste salt,
To drink the blood of sailors,
To watch the waves assault
Mast-high a cliff that shudders
Under their heartless hammers. . . .
Is wind alone at fault?

POISONED DAY

The clouds dripped poisonous dew to spite
A day for weeks looked forward to. True love
Sickened that evening without remedy:
We neither quarrelled, kissed, nor said good-night
But fell asleep, our arms around each other,
And awoke to the gentle hiss of rain on grass
And thrushes calling that the worst was over.

VIRGIN MIRROR

Souls in virginity joined together
   Rest unassailable:
Ours is no undulant fierce rutting fever
   But clear unbroken lunar magic able
   To mirror loves illimitable.

When first we chose this power of being
   I never paused to warn you
What ruinous charms the world was weaving;
   I knew you for a child fostered in virtue
   And swore no hand could hurt you.

Then should I suffer nightmares now
   Lest you, grown somewhat older,
Be lured to accept a worldly where and how,
   Carelessly breathing on the virgin mirror,
   Clouding love's face for ever?

WHAT IS LOVE?

But what is love? Tell me, dear heart, I beg you.
Is it a reattainment of our centre,
A core of trustful innocence come home to?

Is it, perhaps, a first wild bout of being,
The taking of our own extreme measure
And for a few hours knowing everything?

Or what is love? Is it primeval vision
That stars our course with oracles of danger
And looks to death for timely intervention?

SECRET THEATRE

When from your sleepy mind the day's burden
Falls like a bushel sack on a barn floor,
Be prepared for music, for natural mirages
And for night's incomparable parade of colour.

Neither of us daring to assume direction
Of an unforeseen and fiery entertainment,
We clutch hands in the seventh row of the stalls
And watch together, quivering, astonished, silent.

It is hours past midnight now; a flute signals
Far off; we mount the stage as though at random,
Boldly ring down the curtain, then dance out our love:
Lost to the outraged, humming auditorium.

HOW IT STARTED

It started, unexpectedly of course,
At a wild midnight dance, in my own garden,
To which indeed I was not invited:
I read: 'Teen-agers only.'

In the circumstances I stayed away
Until you fetched me out on the tiled floor
Where, acting as an honorary teen-ager,
I kicked off both my shoes.

Since girls like you must set the stage always,
With lonely men for choreographers,
I chose the step, I even called the tune;
And we both danced entranced.

Here the narrator pauses circumspectly,
Knowing me not unpassionate by nature
And the situation far from normal:
Two apple-seeds had sprouted. . . .

Recordable history began again
With you no longer in your late teens
And me socially (once more) my age—
Yet that was where it started.

BRIEF REUNION

Our one foreboding was: we might forget
How strangely close absence had drawn us,
How close once more we must be drawn by parting—
Absence, dark twin of presence!

Nor could such closeness be attained by practice
Of even the most heroic self-deceit:
Only by inbred faculties far wiser
Than any carnal sense—

Progress in which had disciplined us both
To the same doting pride: a stoicism
Which might confuse, at every brief reunion,
Presence with pangs of absence.

And if this pride should overshoot its mark,
Forcing on us a raw indifference
To what might happen when our hearts were fired
By renewed hours of presence?

Could we forget what carnal pangs had seized us
Three summers past in a burst of moonlight,
Making us more possessive of each other
Than either dared concede?—a prescience
Of the vast grief that each sublunary pair
Transmits at last to its chance children
With tears of violence.

THE JUDGES

Crouched on wet shingle at the cove
In day-long search for treasure-trove—
Meaning the loveliest-patterned pebble,
Of any colour imaginable,
Ground and smoothed by a gentle sea—
How seldom, Julia, we agree
On our day's find: the perfect one
To fetch back home when day is done,
Splendid enough to stupefy
The fiercest, most fastidious eye—
Tossing which back we tell the sea:
'Work on it one more century!'

LOVE AND NIGHT

Though your professions, ages and conditions
Might seem to any sober person
Irreconcilable,

Yet still you claim the inalienable right
To kiss in corners and exchange long letters
Patterned with well-pierced hearts.

When judges, dazzled by your blazing eyes,
Mistake you both for Seventh Day Adventists
(Heaven rest their innocent souls!)

You smile impassively and say no word—
The why and how of magic being tabu
Even in courts of Law.

Who could have guessed that your unearthly glow
Conceals a power no judgement can subdue,
Nor act of God, nor death?

Your love is not desire but certainty,
Perfect simultaneity,
Inheritance not conquest;

Long silences divide its delicate phases
With simple absence, almost with unbeing,
Before each new resurgence.

Such love has clues to a riddling of the maze:
Should you let fall the thread, grope for it,
Unawed by the thick gloom.

31

Such love illuminates the far house
Where difficult questions meet their answers
And lies get scoured away.

Your powers to love were forged by Mother Night—
Her perfect discipline of thought and breath—
Sleep is their sustenance.

You prophesy without accessories:
Her words run splashed in light across your walls
For reading as you wake.

But Night, no doubt, has deathless other secrets
Guarded by her unblinking owls against
All clumsy stumbling on them.

CHILD WITH VETERAN

You were a child and I your veteran;
An age of violence lay between us,
Yet both claimed citizenship of the same land
Conversing in our own soft, hidden language,
Often by signs alone.

Our eyelids closed, little by little,
And we fell chained in an enchantment
Heavier than any known or dreamed before,
Groping in darkness for each other's fingers
Lifting them to our lips.

Here brooded power beyond comparison,
Tremendous as a thousand bee-stings
Or a great volley of steel-tipped arrows
With which to take possession of a province
That no one could deny us,
For the swift regeneration of dead souls
And the pride of those undead.

SUPERSTITION

Forget the foolishness with which I vexed you:
Mine was a gun-shy superstition
Surviving from defeat in former loves
And banished when you stood staring aghast
At the replacement of your sturdy lover
By a disconsolate waif.

Blame the foul weather for my aching wounds,
Blame ugly history for my wild fears,
Nor ever turn from your own path; for still
Despite your fancies, your white silences,
Your disappearances, you remain bound
By this unshakeable trust I rest in you.

Go, because inner strength ordains your journey,
Making a necessary occasion seem
No more than incidental. Love go with you
In distillation of all past and future—
You, a clear torrent flooding the mill-race,
Forcing its mill to grind
A coarse grain into flour for angels' bread.

PURIFICATION

'He numbed my heart, he stole away my truth,
He laid hands on my body.
Never had I known ecstasy like that:
I could have flown with him to the world's end
And thought of you no more.'

'Wake, dearest love, here in my own warm arms,
That was a nightmare only.
You kept the wall-side, leaving me the outer,
No demon slid between us to molest you.
This is a narrow bed.'

I would have brought her breakfast on a tray
But she seemed haunted still
By terror that in nine short months, maybe,
A demon's litter, twitching scaly tails
Would hang from either breast.

And still she shuddered inconsolably
All day; our true love-magic
Dwindled and failed. 'He swore to take me
The round of Paris, on his midnight tours,
Fiddling for me to dance.'

Thus to have murdered love even in dream
Called for purification;
And (as the Great Queen yearly did at Paphos)
Down to the sea she trod and in salt water
Renewed virginity.

POWERS UNCONFESSED

Diffidently, when asked who might I be,
I agreed that, yes, I ruled a small kingdom
Though, like yourself, free to wander abroad
Hatless, barefooted and incognito.

Abruptly we embraced—a strange event,
The casual passers-by taking less notice
Than had this been a chance meeting of cousins—
Nor did we argue over protocol.

You, from your queendom, answerable only
To royal virtue, not to a male code,
Knew me for supernatural, like yourself,
And fell at once head over heels in love;
As I also with you—but lamentably
Never confessed what wrathful powers attest
The Roman jealousy of my male genius.

PANDORA

But our escape: to what god did we owe it,
Pandora, my one love?
White-faced we lay, apart and all but dead.

In place of magic had you offered fancy
(Being still a girl and over-credulous)
To honour my poor genius?—
And with your careless innocence of death
Concealed the mischief and those unseen Spites
For long months haunting you and me, your Titan,
Chasing away the honey-bees of love?

Though my acute dream-senses, apprehending,
Warned me with fevers, chills and violences
That the postern gate was forced
And the keep in instant peril,
Why did my eyes stay blind and my ears deaf?

And this escape: to what god did we owe it,
Or to what unborn child?

SOLOMON'S SEAL

Peace is at last confirmed for us:
A double blessing, heavily priced,
Won back as we renew our maiden hearts
In a magic known to ourselves only,
Proof against furious tides of error
And bitter ironies of the self-damned:

Perfect in love now, though not sharing
The customary pillow—and our reasons
Appear shrouded in dark Egyptian dreams
That recreate us as a single being
Wholly in love with love.

Under each pyramid lies inverted
Its twin, the sister-bride to Pharaoh,
And so Solomon's seal bears witness.

Therefore we neither plead nor threaten
As lovers do who have lost faith—
Lovers not riven together by an oath
Sworn on the very brink of birth,
Nor by the penetrative ray of need
Piercing our doubled pyramid to its bed.

All time lies knotted here in Time's caress,
And so Solomon's seal bears witness.

TO PUT IT SIMPLY

Perfect reliance on the impossible
    By strict avoidance of all such conjecture
As underlies the so-called possible:
    That is true love's adventure.

Put it more simply: all the truth we need
    Is ours by curious preknowledge of it—
On love's impossibility agreed,
    Constrained neither by horoscope nor prophet.

Or put it still more simply: all we know
Is that love is and always must be so.

IN THE NAME OF VIRTUE

In the name of Virtue, girl,
Why must you try so hard
In the hard name of Virtue?
Is not such trying, questioning?
Such questioning, doubting?
Such doubting, guessing?
Such guessing, not-knowing?
Such not-knowing, not-being?
Such not-being, death?
Can death be Virtue?

Virtue is from listening
To a private angel,
An angel overheard
When the little-finger twitches—
The bold little-finger
That refused education:
When the rest went to college
And philosophized on Virtue,
It neither went, nor tried.

Knowing becomes doing
When all we need to know
Is how to check our pendulum
And move the hands around
For a needed golden instant
Of the future or past—
Then start time up again
With a bold little-finger
In Virtue's easy name.

TO TELL AND BE TOLD

What is it I most want in all the world?
To be with you at last, alone in the world,
And as I kiss with you to tell and be told.

A child you no more are, yet as a child
You foresaw miracles when no more a child—
So spread a bed for us, to tell and be told.

You wear my promises on rings of gold,
I wear your promise on a chain of gold:
For ever and once more to tell and be told.

THE THEME OF DEATH

Since love is an astonished always
Challenging the long lies of history,
Yesterday when I chose the theme of death
You shook a passionate finger at me:
'Wake from your nightmare! Would you murder love?
Wake from your nightmare!'

No, sweetheart! Death is nightmare when conceived
As God's Last Judgement, or the curse of Time—
Its intransgressible bounds of destiny;
But love is an astonished always
With death as affidavit for its birth
And timeless progress.

What if these tombs and catafalques conspire,
Menacing us with gross ancestral fears,
To dissipate my living truth, and yours,
To induct us into ritual weeping?
Our love remains a still astonished always,
Pure death its witness.

AT THE WELL

To work it out even a thought better
Than ever before—yet a thought rare enough
To raise a sigh of wonder—
That is your art (he said) but mine also
Since first I fell upon the secret
And sighed for wonder that our dry mouths
After a world of travel
Were drawn together by the same spell
To drink at the same well.

Coincidence (she said) continues with us,
Secret by secret,
Love's magic being no more than obstinacy
In love's perfection—
Like the red apple, highest on the tree
Reserved for you by me.

LOGIC

Clear knowledge having come
Of an algebraic queendom,
Compulsive touch and tread
By a public voice dictated
Proclaims renewed loyalty
To a defunct geometry:
Blue-prints of logic—

Logic, tricking the tongue
With its fool's learning,
Prescribed excess,
Devoted emptiness,
With dull heart-burning
For a forgotten peace
For work beyond employment,
For trust beyond allegiance,
For love beyond enjoyment,
For life beyond existence,
For death beyond decease.

They have taken Sun from Woman
And consoled her with Moon;
They have taken Moon from Woman
And consoled her with Seas;
They have taken Seas from Woman
And consoled her with Stars;
They have taken Stars from Woman
And consoled her with Trees;
They have taken Trees from Woman
And consoled her with Tilth;
They have taken Tilth from Woman
And consoled her with Hearth;
They have taken Hearth from Woman
And consoled her with Praise—
Goddess, the robbers' den that men inherit
They soon must quit, going their ways,
Restoring you your Sun, your Moon, your Seas,
Your Stars, your Trees, your Tilth, your Hearth—
But sparing you the indignity of Praise.

THE ACCOMPLICE

Mercury, god of larceny
And banking and diplomacy,
Marks you as his accomplice.

No coins hang from his watch-chain
Where once he used to wear them:
He has done with toys like these.

Would you prove your independence
By entering some Order
Or taking your own life?

He will, be sure, divinely
Revenge the moral fervour
Of your disloyalties.

For his fistful of signed contracts
And million-dollar bank-notes
Bear witness to his credit
With your colleagues, friends, assistants
And your own faithful wife.

FIRST LOVE

Darling, if ever on some night of fever
But with your own full knowledge . . .
Darling, confess how it will be if ever
You violate your true-love pledge
Once offered me unprompted,
Which I reciprocated
Freely, fully and without restraint
Nor ever have abjured since first we kissed?
Will that prove you a liar and me a saint,
Or me a fool and you a realist?

THROUGH A DARK WOOD

Together, trustfully, through a dark wood—
But headed where, unless to the ancient, cruel,
Inescapable, marital pitfall
With its thorny couch for the procreation
Of love's usurpers or interlopers?
Or worse by far, should each be trapped singly
But for true-love's sake gulp down a jealousy
And grief at not having suffered jointly. . . .

Together, through a dark wood, trustfully.

IN THE VESTRY

It is over now, with no more need
For whispers, for brief messages posted
In the chestnut-tree, for blank avoidance
Of each other's eyes at festivals,
For hoarded letters, for blossom-tokens,
For go-betweens or confidants.

Well, are you glad that all is over now?
Be as truthful as you dare.
Posted at last as would-be man and wife
Behaving as the Lord Himself enjoined,
Repudiating your lascivious past,
Each alike swearing never to retrieve it,
Particularly (God knows) with someone else—
Marriage being for procreation only—
Are you both glad and sure that all is over?

WHEN LOVE IS NOT

'Where is love when love is not?'
  Asked the logician.
'We term it Omega Minus,'
  Said the mathematician.

'Does that mean marriage or plain Hell?'
  Asked the logician.
'I was never at the altar,'
  Said the mathematician.

'Is it love makes the world go round?'
  Asked the logician.
'Or you might reverse the question,'
  Said the mathematician.

THE REITERATION

The death of love comes from reiteration:
A single line sung over and over again—
No prelude and no end.

The word is not, perhaps, 'reiteration'—
Nature herself repunctuates her seasons
With the same stars, flowers, fruits—
Though love's foolish reluctance to survive
Springs always from the same mechanical fault:
The needle jumps its groove.

SEMI-DETACHED

Her inevitable complaint or accusation
Whatever the Major does or leaves undone,
Though, being a good wife, never before strangers,
Nor, being a good mother, ever before their child . . .
With no endearments except for cats and kittens
Or an occasional bird rescued from cats . . .
Well, as semi-detached neighbours, with party-walls
Not altogether sound-proof, we overhear
The rare explosion when he retaliates
In a sudden burst of anger, although perhaps
(We are pretty sure) apologizing later
And getting no forgiveness or reply.

He has his own resources—bees and gardening—
And, we conclude, is on the whole happy.
They never sleep together, as they once did
Five or six years ago, when they first arrived,
Or so we judge from washing on their line—
Those double sheets are now for guests only—
But welcome streams of visitors. How many
Suspect that the show put on by both of them,
Of perfect marital love, is apology
In sincere make-believe, for what still lacks?

If ever she falls ill, which seldom happens,
We know he nurses her indefatigably,
But this she greets, we know, with sour resentment,
Hating to catch herself at a disadvantage,
And crawls groaning downstairs to sink and oven.
If he falls ill she treats it as affront—

Except at the time of that car-accident
When he nearly died, and unmistakable grief
Shone from her eyes for almost a whole fortnight,
But then faded . . .
    He receives regular airmail
In the same handwriting, with Austrian stamps.
Whoever sends it, obviously a woman,
Never appears. Those are his brightest moments.
Somehow they take no holidays whatsoever
But are good neighbours, always ready to lend
And seldom borrowing. Our child plays with theirs;
Yet we exchange no visits or confidences.
Only once I penetrated past their hall—
Which was when I fetched him in from the wrecked
    car
And alone knew who had caused the accident.

IAGO

Iago learned from that old witch, his mother,
How to do double murder
On man and woman fallen deep in love;
Lie first to her, then lie again to him,
Make each mistrustful of the honest other.
Guilt and suspicion wear the same sick face—
Two deaths will follow in a short space.

AGAINST WITCHCRAFT

No smile so innocent or angelic
As when she nestled to his wounded heart,
Where the slow poison worked within
And eggs of insane fever incubated . . .

Out, witch, out! Here are nine cloves of garlic
That grew repellent to the Moon's pull;
Here too is every gift you ever gave him,
Wrapped in a silken cloth.
Your four-snake chariot awaits your parting
And here I plant my besom upside down.

MAN OF EVIL

But should I not pity that poor devil,
Such a load of guilt he carries?
He debauched the daughter of his benefactor—
A girl of seventeen—her brother too,
At the same drunken picnic.

Pushes hard drugs, abstains from them himself;
His first wife ended in a mad-house,
The second was found drowned in a forest pool—
The Coroner, observing his distress,
Called for an open verdict.

And so on, oh and so on—why continue?
He complains always of his luckless childhood
And fills commiserating eyes with tears,
The truth is: he was evil from the womb
And both his parents knew it.

He cowers and sponges when his guilt is plain
And his bank-account runs dry.
O, that unalterable black self-pity,
Void of repentance or amendment,
Clouding his Universe!

But who can cast out evil? We can only
Learn to diagnose that natal sickness,
The one known cure for which, so far, is death.
Evil is here to stay unendingly;
But so also is Love.

THE RAFT

Asleep on the raft and forced far out to sea
By an irresistible current:
No good, no good!

O for a sister island! Ships were scarce
In that unhomely latitude,
And he lacked food.

No canoes would row out to his rescue;
No native ever called him brother—
What was brotherhood?

He asked another question: which to choose?
A drowning vision of damnation
Or slow starvation?

Even savages, hungry for his flesh,
Would offer him a happier exit;
And he need not fight.

Yet, having always drifted on the raft
Each night, always without provision,
Loathing each night,

So now again he quaked with sudden terror
Lest the same current, irresistibly
Reversed, should toss him back
Once more on the same shore—
As it did every night.

TOLLING BELL

'*But why so solemn when the bell tolled?*'
'Did you expect me to stand up and caper?'
'*Confess, what are you trying to hide from me?*
Horror of death?'
              'That seventeenth-century
Skeletal effigy in the Church crypt?'
'*Or is it fear, perhaps, of a second childhood?*
Of incurable sickness? Or of a strange someone
Seated in your own chair at your own table?
Or worse, of that chair gone?'
                  'Why saddle me
With your own nightmares?'
                  '*Fear of the other world?*'
'Be your own age! What world exists but ours?'
'*Distaste for funerals?*'
               'Isn't it easier
To play the unweeping corpse than the pall-bearer?'
'*Why so mysterious?*'
            'Why so persistent?'
'*I only asked why you had looked solemn*
When the bell tolled.'
              'Angered, not solemn, angered
By all parochially enforced grief.
Death is a private, ungainsayable act.'
'*Privately, then, what does Death mean to you?*'
'Only love's gentle sigh of consummation,
Which I have little fear of drawing too soon.'

61

THE HERO

Slowly with bleeding nose and aching wrists
After tremendous use of feet and fists
He rises from the dusty schoolroom floor
And limps for solace to the girl next door,
Boasting of kicks and punches, cheers and noise,
And far worse damage done to bigger boys.

BLANKET CHARGE

This fever doubtless comes in punishment
For crimes discovered by your own conscience:
You lie detained here on a blanket charge
    And between blankets lodged.

So many tedious hours of light and dark
To weigh the incriminatory evidence—
With your head somewhat clearer by midday
    Than at its midnight worst.

Ignorance of the Law is no defence
In any Court; but can you plead 'not guilty
Of criminal intent' without a lawyer
    To rise on your behalf?

However long the sentence passed on you,
The term served here will, you assume, be taken
Into consideration; you have proved,
    Surely, a model prisoner?

The worst is finding where your fault lay
In all its pettiness; do you regret
It was not some cardinal, outrageous sin
    That drew crowds to the gibbet?

THE UNCUT DIAMOND

This is ours by natural, not by civil, right:
An uncut diamond, found while picnicking
Beside blue clay here on the open veldt!
It should carve up to a walnut-sized brilliant
And a score of lesser gems.

What shall we do? To be caught smuggling stones
Assures us each a dozen years in gaol;
And who can trust a cutting-agency?
So, do you love me?
                    Or must I toss it back?

THE STRAYED MESSAGE

Characteristic, nevertheless strange:
Something went badly wrong at the Exchange,
And my private message to you, in full detail,
Got broadcast over eleven frequencies
With the usual, though disquieting, consequences
Of a torrential amatory fan-mail.

THE CO-WALKER

I held a poor opinion of myself
While young, but never bettered my opinion
Of all those fellow-fools at school or college
Even by comparison. . . .

Slow lapse of years induced a tolerance,
Even a slow acceptance, of myself—
Which when you fell in love with me amounted
(Though with my tongue still resolutely tied)
To little short of pride.

Pride brought its punishment: to be well haunted
By a co-walker whom eventually
All would-be friends and open enemies
Came to identify and certify
As me, distorting him in anecdotal
Autobiographies.

Love, when you meet him in the newspapers,
In planes, in trains, or at State banquets,
I charge you, disavow his clumsy capers:
Silence him with a cold, unwinking stare
Where he sits opposite you at table;
And let all watchers watch amazed, remarking
On how little you care.

THE RISK

Though there are always doctors who advise
Fools on the care of their own foolish bodies,
And surgeons ready to rush up and set
Well-fractured arms or thighs, never forget
That you are your own body and alone
Can give it a true medical opinion
Drawn not from catalogued analogies
But from a sense of where your danger lies,
And how it obstinately defies the danger.

Your body, though yourself, can play the stranger
As when it falls in love, presuming on
Another's truth and perfect comprehension,
And fails to ask you: dare it run the risk
Of a mild cardiac lesion or slipped disk?

SOMETHING TO SAY

(Dialogue between
Thomas Carlyle and Lewis Carroll)

T.C.   'Would you care to explain
       Why they fight for your books
       With already too many
       Tight-packed on their shelves
       (Many hundreds of thousands
       Or hundreds of millions)
       As though you had written
       Those few for themselves?'

L.C.   'In reply to your query:
       I wrote for one reason
       And only one reason
       (That being my way):
       Not for fame, not for glory,
       Nor yet for distraction,
       But oddly enough
       I had something to say.'

T.C.   'So you wrote for one reason?
       Be damned to that reason!
       It may sound pretty fine
       But relinquish it, pray!
       There are preachers in pulpits
       And urchins in playgrounds
       And fools in asylums
       And beggars in corners
       And drunkards in gutters

And bandits in prisons
With all the right reasons
For something to say.'

TROUBLESOME FAME

To be born famous, as your father's son,
   Is a fate troublesome enough, unless
Like Philip's Alexander of Macedon
   You can out-do him by superb excess
Of greed and profligacy and wantonness.

To become famous as a wonder-child
   Brings no less trouble, with whatever art
You toyed precociously, for Fame had smiled
   Malevolence at your birth . . . Only Mozart
Played on, still smiling from his placid heart.

To become famous while a raw young man
   And lead Fame by the nose, to a bitter end,
As Caesar's nephew did, Octavian
   Styling himself Augustus, is to pretend
Peace in the torments that such laurels lend.

To become famous in your middle years
   For merit not unblessed by accident—
Encountering cat-calls, missiles, jeers and sneers
   From half your uncontrollable parliament—
Is no bad fate, to a good sportsman sent. . . .

But Fame attendant on extreme old age
   Falls best. What envious youth cares to compete
With a lean sage hauled painfully upstage,
   Bowing, gasping, shuffling his frozen feet—
A ribboned hearse parked plainly down the street?

OCCASIONALIA

RESEARCH AND DEVELOPMENT:
CLASSIFIED

We reckon Cooke our best chemist alive
And therefore the least certain to survive
Even by crediting his way-out findings
To our Department boss, Sir Bonehead Clive.

Those Goblins, guessing which of us is what
(And, but for Cooke, we're far from a bright lot),
Must either pinch his know-how or else wipe him.
He boasts himself quite safe. By God, he's not!

In fact, we all conclude that Cooke's one hope
Is neither loud heroics nor soft soap:
Cooke must defect, we warn him, to the Goblins,
Though even they may grudge him enough rope.

THE IMMINENT SEVENTIES

Man's life is threescore years and ten,*
    Which God will surely bless;
Still, we are warned what follows then—
    Labour and heaviness—

And understand old David's grouch
    Though he (or so we're told)
Bespoke a virgin for his couch
    To shield him from the cold. . . .†

Are not all centuries, like men,
    Born hopeful too and gay,
And good for seventy years, but then
    Hope slowly seeps away?

True, a new geriatric art
    Prolongs our last adventures
When eyes grow dim, when teeth depart:
    For glasses come, and dentures—

Helps which these last three decades need
    If true to Freedom's cause:
Glasses (detecting crimes of greed)
    Teeth (implementing laws).

* *Psalms* XC, 10.
† *1 Kings* I, 1–15.

CAROL OF PATIENCE

Shepherds armed with staff and sling,
  Ranged along a steep hillside,
Watch for their anointed King
  By all prophets prophesied—
Sing patience, patience,
Only still have patience!

Hour by hour they scrutinize
  Comet, planet, planet, star,
Till the oldest shepherd sighs:
  'I am frail and he is far.'
Sing patience etc.

'Born, they say, a happy child;
  Grown, a man of grief to be,
From all careless joys exiled,
  Rooted in eternity.'
Sing patience etc.

Then another shepherd said:
  'Yonder lights are Bethlehem;
There young David raised his head
  Destined for the diadem.'
Sing patience etc.

Cried the youngest shepherd: 'There
  Our Redeemer comes tonight,
Comes with starlight on his hair,
  With his brow exceeding bright.'
Sing patience etc.

'Sacrifice no lamb nor kid,
  Let such foolish fashions pass;
In a manger find him hid,
  Breathed upon by ox and ass.'
Sing patience etc.

Dance for him and laugh and sing,
  Watch him mercifully smile,
Dance although tomorrow bring
  Every plague that plagued the Nile!
Sing patience, patience,
Only still have patience!

H

H may be N for those who speak
Russian, although long E in Greek;
And cockneys, like the French, agree
That H is neither N nor E
Nor Hate's harsh aspirate, but meek
And mute as in *Humanity*.

INVITATION TO BRISTOL

'Come as my doctor,
Come as my lawyer,
Or come as my agent
(First practise your lies)
For Bristol is a small town
Full of silly gossip
And a girl gets abashed by
Ten thousand staring eyes.'

'Yes, I'll come as your lawyer
Or as your god-father,
Or even as Father Christmas?—
Not half a bad disguise—
With a jingle of sleigh bells,
A sack full of crackers
And a big bunch of mistletoe
For you to recognize.'

THE PRIMROSE BED

The eunuch and the unicorn
   Walked by the primrose bed;
The month was May, the time was morn,
   Their hearts were dull as lead.

'Ah, unicorn', the eunuch cried,
   'How tragic is our Spring,
With stir of love on every side,
   And loud the sweet birds sing.'

Then, arm and foreleg intertwined,
   Both mourned their cruel fate—
The one was single of his kind,
   The other could not mate.

POEM: A REMINDER

Capital letters prompting every line,
Lines printed down the centre of each page,
Clear spaces between groups of these, combine
In a convention of respectable age
To mean: 'Read carefully. Each word we chose
Has rhythm and sound and sense. This is not prose.'

poem: a reminder

capitallett

        -ers prompting ev

                -eryline lines printed down the
                cen
                -tre of each page clear

                spaces between

                groups of these combine in a con

v

   e

      n

         t

           i

              o

                 n

                of respectable age to mean read

care

                -fully each word we chose has

                          rhythm and
                          sound and
                          sense this is

notprose

THE STRANGLING IN
MERRION SQUARE

None ever loved as Molly loved me then,
    With her whole soul, and yet
How might the patientest of Irishmen
    Forgive, far less forget
Her long unpaid and now unpayable debt?
There's scarce a liveried footman in the Square
But can detail you how and when and where.

SONG: THE SUNDIAL'S LAMENT

(Air: The Groves of Blarney)

Since much at home on
My face and gnomon,
The sun refuses
Daylight to increase;
Yet certain powers dare
Miscount my hours there
Though sun and shadow still collogue in peace.

These rogues aspire
To act Hezekiah
For whom Isaiah
In a day of trial,
All for delaying
His end by praying
Turned back the shadow
On my honest dial.

Nay, Sirs, though willing
To abase the shilling
From noble twelvepence
To the half of ten,
Pray go no further
On this path of murther:
If hours be Dismalised,
Sure, I'm finished then.

ANTORCHA Y CORONA, 1968

Píndaro no soy, sino cabellero
De San Patricio; y nuestro santo
Siglos atrás se hizo mejicano.

Todos aquí alaban las mujeres
Y con razón, como divinos seres—
Por eso entrará en mis deberes

A vuestra Olimpiada mejicana
El origen explicar de la corona:
En su principio fué femenina. . . .

Antes que Hercules con paso largo
Metros midiera para el estadio
Miles de esfuerzos así alentado—

Ya antes, digo, allí existia
Otra carrera mas apasionada
La cual presidia la diosa Hera.

La virgen que, a su fraternidad
Supero con maxima velocidad
Ganaba el premio de la santidad:

La corona de olivo. . . . Me perdonará
El respetable, si de Atalanta
Sueño, la corredora engañada

Con tres manzanas, pero de oro fino. . . .
Y si los mitos griegos hoy resumo
Es que parecen de acuerdo pleno,

A la inventora primeval del juego,
A la Santa Madre, más honores dando
Que no a su portero deportivo.

En tres cientas trece Olimpiadas
Este nego la entrada a las damas
Amenazandolas, ai, con espadas!

Aquí, por fin, brindemos por la linda
Enriqueta de Basilio: la primera
Que nos honra con antorcha y corona. *

---

* This poem, with its English translation, was read at the
Mexican Cultural Olympiads and awarded the Gold Medal
for Poetry.

TORCH AND CROWN, 1968

(English translation of the foregoing)

No Pindar, I, but a poor gentleman
Of Irish race. Patrick, our learned saint,
Centuries past made himself Mexican.

All true-bred Mexicans idolize women
And with sound reason, as divine beings,
I therefore owe it you as my clear duty

At your Olympics, here in Mexico,
To explain the origin of the olive crown:
In the Golden Age women alone could wear it.

Long before Hercules with his huge stride
Paced out the circuit of a stadium,
Provoking men to incalculable efforts,

Long, long before, in Argos, had been run
Even more passionately, a girls' foot race
Under the watchful eye of Mother Hera.

The inspired runner who outstripped all rivals
Of her sorority and finished first
Bore off that coveted and holy prize—

The olive crown. Ladies and gentlemen,
Forgive me if I brood on Atalanta,
A champion quarter-miler tricked one day

By three gold apples tumbled on her track;
And if I plague you with these ancient myths
That is because none of them disagrees

In paying higher honours to the foundress
Of all competitive sport—the Holy Mother—
Than to her sportive janitor, Hercules.

Three hundred and thirteen Olympic Games
Hercules held, though warning off all ladies,
Even as audience, with the naked sword!

So homage to Enriqueta de Basilio
Of Mexico, the first girl who has ever
Honoured these Games with torch and olive crown!

THE AWAKENING

Just why should it invariably happen
That when the Christian wakes at last in Heaven
He finds two harassed surgeons watching by
In white angelic smocks and gloves, and why
Looking so cross and (as three junior nurses
Trundle the trolley off with stifled curses)
Why joking that the X-ray photograph
Must have been someone else's—what a laugh!—?

Now they may smoke. . . . A message from downstairs
Says: 'Matron says, God's due soon after Prayers.'

ARMISTICE DAY, 1918

What's all this hubbub and yelling,
  Commotion and scamper of feet,
With ear-splitting clatter of kettles and cans,
  Wild laughter down Mafeking Street?

O, those are the kids whom we fought for
  (You might think they'd been scoffing our rum)
With flags that they waved when we marched off to
    war
  In the rapture of bugle and drum.

Now they'll hang Kaiser Bill from a lamp-post,
  Von Tirpitz they'll hang from a tree. . . .
We've been promised a 'Land Fit for Heroes'—
  What heroes we heroes must be!

And the guns that we took from the Fritzes,
  That we paid for with rivers of blood,
Look, they're hauling them down to Old Battersea
    Bridge
  Where they'll topple them, souse, in the mud!

But there's old men and women in corners
  With tears falling fast on their cheeks,
There's the armless and legless and sightless—
  It's seldom that one of them speaks.

And there's flappers gone drunk and indecent
  Their skirts kilted up to the thigh,
The constables lifting no hand in reproof
  And the chaplain averting his eye. . . .

89

When the days of rejoicing are over,
   When the flags are stowed safely away,
They will dream of another wild 'War to End Wars'
   And another wild Armistice day.

But the boys who were killed in the trenches,
   Who fought with no rage and no rant,
We left them stretched out on their pallets of mud
   Low down with the worm and the ant.